D1189169

Cell Mates

Simon Gray was born in 1936. He began his writing
career with *Colmain* (1963), the first of five novels, all
published by Faber. He was the author of many plays for
TV and radio, also films, including the 1987 adaptation
of J. L. Carr's *A Month in the Country*, and TV films
including *Running Late*, *After Pilkington* (winner of the
Prix Italia) and the Emmy Award-winning *Unnatural
Pursuits*. He wrote more than thirty stage plays, among
them *Butley* and *Otherwise Engaged* (which both
received *Evening Standard* Awards for Best Play), *Close
of Play*, *The Rear Column*, *Quartermaine's Terms*, *The
Common Pursuit*, *Hidden Laughter*, *The Late Middle
Classes* (winner of the Barclay's Best Play Award), *Japes*,
The Old Masters (his ninth play to be directed by Harold
Pinter) and *Little Nell*, which premiered at the Theatre
Royal Bath in 2007, directed by Peter Hall. *Little Nell*
was first broadcast on BBC Radio 4 in 2006, and *Missing
Dates* in 2008. In 1991 he was made BAFTA Writer of
the Year. His acclaimed works of non-fiction are *An
Unnatural Pursuit*, *How's That for Telling 'Em*, *Fat
Lady?*, *Fat Chance*, *Enter a Fox*, *The Smoking Diaries*,
The Year of the Jouncer, *The Last Cigarette* and *Coda*.
With Hugh Whitemore he adapted his *Smoking Diaries*
for the stage: *The Last Cigarette* was directed by Richard
Eyre in 2009. Simon Gray was appointed CBE in the
2005 New Year's Honours for his services to Drama and
Literature. He died in August 2008.

For more information please visit
www.simongray.org.uk

SIMON GRAY

Cell Mates

FABER & FABER

First published in 1995
by Faber and Faber Limited
74–77 Great Russell Street, London WC1B 3DA

Reprinted 2017

Typeset by Country Setting, Kingsdown, Kent CT14 8ES
Printed in England by CPI Group (UK) Ltd, Croydon, CR0 4YY

A CIP record for this book is available from the British Library

978-0-571-34602-8

FSC
www.fsc.org
MIX
Paper from
responsible sources
FSC® C013604

2 4 6 8 10 9 7 5 3 1

Cell Mates was first presented at the Yvonne Arnaud Theatre, Guildford, on 17 January 1995 and transferred to the Albery Theatre, London, on 16 February 1995. The cast, in order of appearance, was as follows:

Sean Bourke Rik Mayall
George Blake Stephen Fry
Philip / Viktor Paul Mooney
Miranda / Zinaida Carole Nimmons
Sparrow / Stan Sam Dastor

Directed by Simon Gray
Lighting Designer Mick Hughes
Set Designer Eileen Diss

Cell Mates was revived at Hampstead Theatre, London, on 30 November 2017. The cast, in order of appearance, was as follows:

Sean Bourke Emmet Byrne
George Blake Geoffrey Streatfeild
Philip / Viktor Danny Lee Wynter
Miranda / Zinaida Cara Horgan
Sparrow / Stan Philip Bird

Director Edward Hall
Designer Michael Pavelka
Lighting Designer Rick Fisher
Sound Designer John Leonard
Composer Simon Slater

Characters

Sean Bourke

George Blake

Philip

Miranda

Sparrow

Zinaida

Stan

Viktor

CELL MATES

Act One

Bourke's office in Wormwood Scrubs. There are boxes of magazines on the floor. Bourke has his feet on the table, looking through a pile of typescripts. He has a pot of tea beside him, a mug in his hand. He picks out one typescript, begins to read.

Bourke (*aloud*)
   'Oh, spare a thought ye people there
   For all of us who dwell in here.
   Sinners all, we must endure
   Until again our souls are pure.

   And then the gates will open wide
   And out we'll go from dark inside . . .'

Blake enters, unseen by Bourke. Stands watching him.

   'To dash about the valleys green
   And by our loved ones brightly seen
   As we clasp them to our pounding hearts
   Our wives and children, those better parts
   Whom we left in shame, our heads held low,
   But now return to, though the healing's slow.

   And listen judges, juries all –'

Bourke breaks off with a laugh, drops typescript back on table.

   And listen judges, juries all –
   Listen when my heart does call!
   Oh pray don't sentence me to poems so bad
   That listening at them makes me –

He is suddenly aware of Blake.

Blake Glad? Mad?

Bourke No, sad, I think it was going to be. It was written by a young house-burglar. Doing five years for grievous bodily harm. If I publish it he'll be able to show it to his wife and two daughters – it'll give him and them a lot of pleasure and pride, more than anything else he's done in his life, almost. That's what's sad.

Blake So you'll publish it?

Bourke I'm the editor of the Wormwood Scrubs magazine, sir! The world expects the highest literary standards from me – I can't let my personal feelings get in the way of true judgement, can I?

Blake In other words, you're going to publish it.

Bourke He's six foot three, he has a violent temper, he believes on the basis of this that he has a great, great talent – would you care to deliver the rejection slip yourself, sir?

Blake No. But then I wouldn't be fool enough to reject it, my standards not being as high as yours.

Bourke Then I compromise! I publish it as long as he changes the title.

Blake Which is?

Bourke (*picks up typescript*) 'All is Not Lost if All is Forgiven'.

Blake And what would you change it to?

Bourke (*thinks*) What about 'An Unpublishable Poem by Steve Lewis'.

Blake I think that tells the whole story.

Bourke Good. Because that's what we care about –
telling the whole story.

Blake These are the rejects, are they?

Bourke They are indeed, sir.

Blake Ah, well, in that case . . .

Bourke It's a pleasure to meet you at last, Mr Blake.
You're something of a celebrity in this institution, I expect
you realise. To my knowledge almost every fellow convict
thinks you're a national disgrace.

Blake Thank you, Mr Bourke. Becoming a national
disgrace is the reward of a lifetime's endeavour. I've
earned every one of my forty years.

Bourke (*laughs*) I think you know what I meant, that
your *sentence* – is – a national disgrace. A disgrace to this
nation, anyway. It's not my nation, thank God – but to
what do I owe the – the privilege?

Blake I asked my custodian if I could pop in for a
moment. To pick up a copy of the last issue. He's having
a cup of coffee with a colleague. If he wants me he'll
blow on his whistle. I wanted to pick up a copy of the
last issue.

Bourke You don't want to read it. But why not consider
writing for it? Autobiographical piece. Telling your side
of the story. Then I might enjoy reading it myself.

Blake Thank you, but you'd be disappointed. I write
badly. Very stilted. Over-guarded, probably. A habit
acquired in my profession.

Bourke Then tell me about the Turk.

Blake Oh, the Turk! There's nothing much to tell there.

Bourke It's made you a legend.

Blake A legend *and* a celebrity. With thirty-three years to go. If I keep up this level of achievement –

Bourke You could end up editing the in-house magazine. Your own teapot. A table to put your feet on. Peace and quiet. A room with a view, But what happened with the Turk, Mr Blake? Is it true you disarmed him, threw him over your shoulder, pinned him to the wall while you talked to him in Turkish –

Blake Only the last bit's true. He ran amok in the canteen – he had a sudden fit, you see, at the thought that he'd never see his family again, never see Turkey again. So while he was shouting and baying and swearing and threatening and waving his knife I tried to explain to him in his own language that if he calmed down and gave me the knife, all was not lost, all might be forgiven. Anyway, that he'd have a decent chance of getting home eventually.

Bourke So he gave you the knife – and went quietly over to the guards.

Blake Who'd maintained a respectful distance between themselves and his knife. He bowed in submission –

Bourke – whereupon they probably kicked and beat and throttled the – bejesus out of him.

Blake I expect so. But that he'll survive.

Bourke I've seen you walking with the other two – Dick and Nigel – the other prisoners of conscience, as you're called. Also a national disgrace – thrown in jail for marching against the bomb! And Nigel married, with children – (*Suddenly realising.*) Sorry. I was forgetting. You're married yourself, aren't you? And with children.

Blake (*briskly*) I've told my wife to get a divorce as soon as possible. Anyway, I won't be walking with them much longer, he's out in a few months, Nigel. Home to his wife, Annie. And so's Dick too. I don't mean that Dick's off home to Nigel's wife Annie.

Bourke It's a lovely thought, though – and you can just see her, their Annie, without ever having seen her – the type – so English –

Blake – the two short-term prisoners of conscience sharing –

Bourke – and her fitting them both in in the middle of the bed, Nigel on one shoulder, Dick on the other – then off on their marches, their picnics. God, I love the middle-class English.

Blake Careful. I was almost one myself, remember. (*Laughs again.*)

Bourke Makes a change to have someone to enjoy a harmless joke with.

Blake And it is harmless! Nobody could have more respect –

Bourke – for Annie –

Blake – and her jailbird lovers. Perhaps when you're out you'll join them. But will she wait for me?

Bourke You know, the odd thing is, Mr Blake, I've been expecting this kind of conversation with you. Imagining it, even.

Blake Yes, that is an odd thing. Because so have I, Mr Bourke.

Bourke You know, I've seen you often in the cafeteria, in the courtyard –

Blake I've seen you seeing me. But it's been difficult to make the approach. A matter of – of – (*then with surprise*) shyness, perhaps.

They laugh again. There is a pause.

Bourke Will you have a cup of tea?

Blake I'd love one but I don't think I'll be allowed the time. Tell me, Mr Bourke, when *do* you get out?

Bourke Not soon enough. A year or so.

Blake That means I have a friend for a year or so. So I hope.

Bourke You have a friend for at least a year. Count on it.

Blake And Nigel's wife aside, what will you do when you're out and about again?

Bourke Try my hand at writing. I'm already trying my hand but – (*Shakes his head.*) The atmosphere here isn't conducive. So the first thing I'll do is get myself home. Back to Dublin, and among my own people again. And who knows – perhaps being there'll help me to become a fine and successful author, the genuine article. So there I'll be, strutting along the streets of Dublin – laughing, joking, singing songs in the pub – a famous book or two behind me – another one in my head – (*Laughs.*)

Blake Well, why not? It could happen. If you make it happen.

Bourke Yes, well – it's a hope I have to cling to. I've wasted too many years of myself. On what? Being a petty criminal. What's worse, a failed petty criminal. Well, there's going to be no more of that, because I'll tell you something, Mr Blake, whatever my record shows, I'm a man of intelligence. Resources and intelligence. Believe me.

Blake I do. I know it. From what I've heard about you. From what I've heard from you.

Bourke Thank you. (*Little pause.*) Well, as for you, Mr Blake – I know what you want, of course.

Blake Yes.

Bourke Any idea how to get it? I mean, what about your, um, foreign friends?

Blake Oh, the Russians, you mean? What can they do? Fly down in a helicopter, pluck me up and away to my freedom? Well, they haven't done it so far, have they? And I don't think I can wait around for them too much longer. (*Little pause.*) It did cross my mind that someone with outside contacts might find me some sort of – of professional group –

Bourke A gang you're after, are you? How much could you pay them?

Blake I could raise a little – not much. There's my family to provide for – the mortgage, children's education –

Bourke So you're looking for a gang to spring you, with almost no money to pay them.

Blake Yes, it does seem preposterous, doesn't it, when you put it like that. They don't exist –

Bourke Oh yes they do. And you wouldn't have to pay them – the government would pay them for you. In return for information received. The Home Office would know about your plans before you did. Then you'd be off to a maximum security prison where you'd never get a chance at a human conversation again. Not once in the rest of your thirty-five years.

Blake I see. Thank you. Thank you for telling me.

Bourke What you need is a single fella. One who knows the insides here, and a bit about the workings of the outsides, too.

Blake I see. But – well, how do I find this fella? This single fella.

Bourke I don't know, Mr Blake. He'd have to be a fella you could trust. But I tell you what – I'll keep an eye – my mind and my memory and my eye – open.

Blake That's very good of you, Mr Bourke. Thank you. My name's George, by the way. *George* Blake.

He holds out his hand.

Bourke And mine's Sean. Sean Bourke. Sean Alphonsus Bourke.

Taking hand. A whistle sounds.

Blake Ah, I'm being summoned. I'll be seeing you, Sean.

Bourke You will, George. You'll be seeing me.

Blake Thank you.

Blake exits.

Bourke Well, why not, Sean? Why not?

Lights.

SCENE TWO

Winter 1966. About eight in the evening. Bedsitter in London: a bed, a kitchenette, door to bathroom off.
    Blake is sitting in his underwear, slumped. Clothes are scattered around him. Other clothes neatly piled beside him. The television is on. From television, ballroom dancing, music. Commentator's voice.

Commentator And this is Linda and Sidney from Luton, third in last year's finals. And now Frederick and Alison from Purley – this is the first time they've competed. Frederick's a schoolteacher and Alison is a social worker. Ah, and here's Herbert with his new partner Daphne from Sidcup. Daphne has taken over from Marguerite, who has given birth to twins since last year's competition – but doesn't she look cool? Not a sign of nerves – ah, and now Harold and Lynette, in some ways the most remarkable couple on the floor –

Blake gets up, totters to set, turns it off. Commentator's voice fades down.

Lynette is a deft mover – (*Voice becomes almost inaudible, vanishes.*)

Blake (*stands unsteadily, staring at television*) What, deaf mute? Lynette is a deaf mute? That can't be right. It must be my head, Sean. (*Looks around, sees room is empty.*) I must be hearing things – (*Begins to make his way back to chair.*) Sean, Sean, where are you?

Bourke enters.

Where have you been, where have you been, Sean? Why did you leave me?

Bourke George, George, I've been stashing the car. I told you I was going to. Don't you remember? I've put it in Harvist Road, looks like all the others in the street, it could be there for years and –

Blake What? What are you talking about, Sean?

Bourke The car, George. It's in Harvist Road, George –

Blake Why was that on television?

Bourke Television? There's been something about you on television?

Blake No, no, not me, the music. And the grinning faces in chiffon. And a voice like treacle telling us about a deaf mute. In a ballroom competition. That sort of thing.

Bourke You've gone feverish. I was afraid you would. Come on, George, let's get you to bed.

Blake No, no, Sean – (*Pushing Bourke away.*) Something I haven't finished. Something I have to do. (*Stares around agitatedly, then looks down at himself.*) Oh yes. Get dressed. I've got to get myself out of uniform – into decent clothes. Street clothes. Where are my decent street clothes? I need them.

Bourke They're here, George, on the bed. (*Picks up pile of neatly folded clothes.*) So let's get to it, eh? (*Picks up trousers.*) Lift your leg – and the other one – that's a good fit now, that's a good fit, George, considering they're from off the peg and guesswork. Arm now, sleeve a bit short – and the other one – (*Buttoning up shirt.*) Well, the collar's all right, a little snug – (*Stands back, surveying him.*) What's it like, too snug, George?

Blake Yes, snug. Nice and snug. Thank you, Sean. Togging me up –

Bourke Time to tog you up inside. Here. Wrap yourself around this.

He opens bottle, hands it to Blake.

Blake Do you think I should?

Bourke Not if you don't want to.

Blake I don't know what I want, Sean. There's something – something I always want. But I don't think it's this. (*Lifts bottle to lips, takes a swig.*)

Bourke No, no, steady, George –

He snatches bottle back from Blake.

A few sips, a few careful sips –

Blake Mmm?

He stands swaying, lurches sideways suddenly.

Bourke Oh, Jesus! Oh, *Jesus*!

Catches Blake. There is a ring on the doorbell.

Oh, Jesus! That's not the signal! Three short and one long is –

Another ring.

(*Dragging Blake towards lavatory door.*) Come on. Let's get you to the toilet.

Blake (*stumbling eagerly towards it*) Oh, the toilet! Yes. Yes, please – that's what I need.

There are three short rings. One long.

Bourke Ah, that's it! Thank God. Don't worry, it's only Nigel and Annie – or Dick –

Puts Blake into a chair, hurries to door, opens it.

Blake Who is it? Who is it?

Bourke Actually, it's Philip!

Blake (*in feeble alarm*) Philip? Who's Philip?

Philip Gosh, sorry, Nigel told me the signal but I forgot –

Bourke I wasn't expecting you just yet.

Philip I know, but I couldn't resist. So, there you are, Mr Blake . . . Mr George Blake himself. What a great moment for true British justice . . . Miranda's not here yet, then?

Bourke Miranda's just your wife, Philip.

Blake Miranda – Miranda – who's Miranda? Sean – Sean, I thought nobody knew where we were except Nigel and Annie. And Dick.

Bourke Philip's a great friend of Nigel's and Annie's and Dick's too. In fact, he gave some money to the cause.

Blake The cause, what cause?

Bourke You, George – the cause of you. I needed financial support, you see. While I was on the job. Food and accommodation. And for renting the car. Philip was very generous.

Philip Well, I gave what I could. Nothing on the scale of Nigel and Annie. Or Dick even. (*To Bourke.*) She'll be here in a minute, I'm sure.

Blake Who?

Philip Well, Miranda.

Blake Miranda? Who's Miranda?

Bourke She's the wife, George, that's all.

Blake The wife, *the* wife, whose wife? This can't be real, can't be, must be my head –

Bourke Rest your head, George, don't upset yourself, no need, it's all under control –

Blake Whose wife? (*Almost screaming.*) Whose wife?

Bourke His.

Philip Well, actually she's not my wife, Sean, didn't you realise that? But she would be if she wanted to get married. She's taking her time, you see. Finding out. She's very independent. Quite right too. Actually, to tell you the truth, we're going through a bit of a bad patch at the moment.

Bourke Oh no, Philip, not again.

Philip Anyway, please don't be put off by her manner. Obviously you're a rather awkward proposition for her, professionally, she has to protect her interests –

Blake (*gapes at Bourke*) What professionally? What?

Bourke (*evasively*) She's a lovely girl, George. With a good heart.

He gives Philip a warning look, which Philip doesn't notice.

Blake Good heart? Good heart?

Philip She's not doing it just for me, you know. She's doing it for you too. She feels as strongly about you morally as I do. Though we can't go all the way with you, ideologically speaking, we both respect – no, speaking for myself, more than respect, I admire the courage with which you've acted on your principles. As you believed, so did you live. And so shall I write to that effect.

Blake Write, write, you'll write –

Philip Yes, I'm a journalist.

Blake (*in a moan*) A journalist. Yes, please. And a camera, could we have some cameras here too? I could get back into my prison garb –

Bourke George!

Blake – and pose with the police before they take me back to jail.

Bourke Philip's not that sort of journalist, George. Will you trust me, trust me, will you –

Philip I write on matters of conscience. Strictly matters of conscience.

Bourke Conscience. There. You see.

Philip That's how I met Nigel and Annie. And old Dick too. Covering all the CND rallies – the marches, Aldermaston for the *New Statesman* – so I wasn't sent to jail. Like Nigel and Dick. Shameful. Shameful. Sent to jail for their beliefs. Just like you. I often wish I had been – (*Laughs.*) Well, just for the eighteen months. So I could have met people like you.

Bourke There aren't any people like George, Philip.

Blake No, I'm very special. I wasn't doing eighteen months. I was doing forty years. And probably will again. Sean! Sean!

He clutches Bourke's arm.

I'm sorry, Sean. Just testing. For reality.

Bourke I'm real enough for our purposes, George. You're safe. And you'll be sound. I promise it.

Blake Thank you, Sean. But there's a question hanging about somewhere in my head. About – about – the girl with a good heart, is that it?

Bourke George, you'll oblige me by sitting down. And stop fretting, eh?

There is a pause.

Philip (*to Bourke*) Am I allowed to know how you did it?

Blake Don't tell him, Sean! You mustn't.

Bourke It's no secret, George. It'll be public knowledge tomorrow. If it isn't already. The how of it.

Blake Yes, yes, the how of it, but not the who of it – you mustn't tell him who.

Bourke George, George, he knows the who. He's looking at the who and asking about the how.

Blake But he's not to tell anybody who –

Bourke He knows that, George.

Blake Does he? Do you? Do you know that?

Philip Yes, of course I know it. I mean – I mean, well I'm not actually mad. (*Laughs slightly.*) If they find out it's Sean, they'll find out about Nigel and Annie and Dick and Miranda and me. And we'll go to jail.

Bourke There. That's settled then. Eh, George?

Blake The wife, the wife – what was it he said about the wife?

Bourke That they're going through a bad patch, George, and they're not actually married. Now, Philip, you wanted to know how we did it. Just as I planned. George sawed through some bars, I threw my rope ladder over the wall. George climbed up it. George fell down the other side. That bit I didn't plan. His missing his footing.

Blake He tried to catch me. Went through his arms.

Bourke Broke the fall though, George.

Blake Yes. Broke the fall, Sean. Thank you.

Philip And then you just got into the car? And drove here?

Bourke That's it. That's the whole story, Philip.

Philip But that's – that's – (*Laughing.*) It's like something out of a – a comic book!

Bourke Comic book!

Philip Sawing through bars, a rope ladder –

Bourke (*suddenly angry*) A comic book! That's what you think, is it?

Philip Well, so simple –

Bourke Here. Here, you listen to this! Listen to this!

Bourke goes to table, picks up tape recorder, winds it back, presses 'Play' button.

Bourke (*voice on tape recorder*) Traffic lights to take notice of. The real bugger is at Halcyon Road where they take two minutes to change from red to green and about twenty seconds to change back to red – you could be stuck for six to eight minutes –

Bourke turns off recorder, stares at Philip, points to piles of tapes.

Look at them, hours and hours of them, me walking around the Scrubs, driving around the Scrubs, detailing all the details, until I knew exactly when, exactly where, to the minute – one chance, I had one chance for George. It took work, work, work to work it out. The precise minute. What does it matter that it was with a hacksaw, a rope ladder, a hired car if it was the only way? It was the precise minute that mattered. Comic book – comic book – you get that in your comic books, do you? Eh, Philip?

Blake See this man here? He's a genius. Don't you understand that? Sean Bourke. Sean Alphonsus Bourke. Sheer genius. And a great gentleman. Do you understand? Or don't you? Eh? (*Aggressively, if faintly.*)

Philip Yes, look – I'm terribly sorry – the last thing I meant – I can't tell you how much I admire you. Both of you.

Blake There's only one of you at last, Sean, thank God. So my head's clearing at last. (*Looks at Philip.*) Who did you say you are? There's almost none of *you* that I can see. Oh, that's it! I've got it now, his wife, his Miranda, she's against me professionally, isn't that what he said, Sean? What does that mean?

Philip Only that seeing you professionally puts her in a dodgy –

Doorbell rings once.

That's probably her.

Bourke It's not the signal.

Philip I can't – can't remember whether I remembered to pass it on – the signal –

Bourke Oh God, Philip!

Doorbell rings again.

Well, answer the door. If it's not her, send them away.

Philip (*goes apprehensively to the door*) I'm not good –
not very good – at lying, I'm afraid. (*Goes to door,
hesitates.*) I'll – I'll –

Blake Not very good at lying? Who are these people?
What's going on? Sean!

Bourke (*goes to stand in front of Blake.*) Sit down,
George. Not another word from you. Not a word. (*To
Philip.*) You – open the door . . . open the door.

Philip (*opens the door*) Oh, Miranda, love, thank God!

Miranda enters, carrying a black bag.

Bourke George – Miranda's a doctor, George.

Blake What? A doctor! But I told you – no doctors. No
doctors. I told you –

Bourke I know, George. But a head injury's a head injury
– I couldn't take the risk.

Blake She's the risk you shouldn't have taken.

Miranda Look, do you want to see me or don't you?

Bourke (*coaxingly*) Miranda – Miranda, love –

Miranda Dr Joseph, if you please. (*To Bourke and
Blake.*) And I've never seen you two before in my life.

Bourke Dr Joseph, right, Miranda, but whatever he says,
he needs you to look at him – he fell off the wall of the
Scrubs –

Miranda That's already more than I need to know about
the cause of his injury. Now, do I examine you, or don't I?

Bourke George! You'll do it for me.

Blake As you're here – and been put to such trouble – I would be greatly obliged, (*smiles charmingly*) Dr Joseph.

Miranda You've drunk alcohol from the smell of your breath. Bloody stupid.

Examining Blake's forehead.

Nasty but superficial. Should heal quickly.

Checks Blake's eyes and reflexes.

You're probably in shock and have got mild concussion. (*To Bourke.*) But he's right, a head injury's a head injury. You should go to a hospital for an X-ray.

Bourke But Miranda, he can't possibly go to a hospital.

Philip No, of course he can't, Miranda, love.

Miranda I've given my professional opinion. Whether it's taken is not my responsibility. Then I suppose I'll have to give you a shot of penicillin. (*Takes syringe out of bag.*)

Blake What? I hate needles. They – they –

Bourke You've got to have it, George.

He begins to roll up Blake's sleeve.

Miranda No, I need a buttock.

Bourke Come on, George.

Blake (*trying to push Philip away*) I can do it – I can do it – (*Tries futilely to undo his belt.*)

Bourke No, you can't, George. Leave it to me.

Philip supports Blake. Bourke undoes Blake's trousers, pulls down his underpants, bends him over.

Go on now, George – a bit lower – bend over.

Blake is bent over, held by Philip and Bourke, buttocks exposed.

Miranda (*jabs syringe*) There. (*As she packs up.*) I've one last thing to say. What this man needs above all is sleep. Plenty of it. If he gets it, he shouldn't require further medical treatment. Which he won't be getting from me, anyway. Please remember I've never seen any of you before. And I shan't be seeing any of you again –

Philip You've been absolutely wonderful, love.

Miranda (*to Philip*) And that includes you.

Philip What? Oh, Miranda, love – (*Takes her arm.*) You can't mean it!

Miranda (*snatching her arm away*) Oh, yes, I mean it. How could you, how could you let me? Did you give a single thought to my future?

Philip But Miranda love – Dr Joseph – I didn't make you come. It was your choice, your own personal choice.

Miranda You told me where he was and how he was. You told me he needed help. So you knew I wouldn't have any choice – none at all.

Philip But we agreed we'd always tell each other everything. And we're always saying people can't go through life not knowing things deliberately. The truth is the truth, facts are facts. It's no good being angry at all the injustices in our society, including him – (*pointing to Blake*) if it's just a matter of principle, but when it comes to the actual living and breathing victim – George Blake himself – the George Blake who needs something practical done for him – not just slogans and high-minded debates – but there, *that* George Blake –

Miranda Why do you keep on saying his name? Are you trying to ruin my life, is that what this is about? Because you resent my independence, my having a career – so you'd rather see me struck off and go to jail –

Bourke Miranda, darling, we'll never mention your name. Even if we're caught, we'll never mention it, will we, George?

Philip You see? You're just overwrought, love. So why don't you go back to the flat, have a cup of tea and an aspirin and lie down – and when I get back, we'll talk the whole thing through.

Miranda When you get back to the flat, you'll find all your things outside the door. You're moving out, Philip.

Philip Oh, no, I'm not! No, I'm not! For one thing, it's my flat, I own the lease.

Miranda I'll buy it from you. Don't worry, I'll give you a fair price.

Philip There isn't a fair price. I'll never get another flat like 21E Phildeep Gardens for that money – not with a patio and access to the gardens. If you really want us to separate, you're the one who'll have to move out. Back to Mummy and Daddy – the Brigadier and his lady wife and their three dogs and bring back hanging and keep out the blacks and as for that swine, George Blake, let him . . . let him . . .

Miranda (*to Blake and Bourke*) I suppose I should be grateful to you. It's because of you I've found out what kind of man he really is.

She makes to open the door, as doorbell rings.

Bourke No, don't open it!

Miranda has already opened the door.

Sparrow (*entering, to Philip*) Sorry to call at this late hour, but better than a dawn raid, eh? Sparrow and Week. Property Management Agents. I'm the Sparrow.

During this Bourke has bent over Blake, not yet taken in by Sparrow.

Philip It's not us. Nothing to do with us. Him you want, I expect. (*Gestures towards Bourke.*) Well, darling, we'd better be going or we'll be late. The theatre . . .

Miranda (*pushing past Sparrow*) Yes. *Much Ado.* Zeffirelli's. At the Old Vic.

Sparrow Well, do enjoy it.

Miranda Thank you.

Sparrow (*looks at clipboard in his hand*) Well, the him I want is O'Brien, Mr O'Brien?

He looks towards Bourke, who turns.

Bourke (*assuming a much stronger Irish accent*) Evening, sir. How can I help you, sir?

Sparrow I'm here on behalf of the landlord. Need to look around, make sure everything's roughly as it ought to be.

Bourke I hope you don't mind being quick about it, sir. My brother here (*stepping aside*) was told down at the hospital he needed a good, long lay-down.

Sparrow Oh, I see.

Bourke But you should see t'other fellows, as they say, eh, Seamus?

Sparrow Oh. It was a fight then, was it?

Bourke Well, he's a peace-loving man, sir, is Seamus, it takes a lot to set him blazin', but down the pub this noon a couple of ill-advised boyos took it on themselves to say somethin' inflamin' 'bout te motter-country, sir, and that did it, d'int it, Seamus?

Blake Yes.

Bourke Take it from me, sir, they'll be careful what t'ey say about Motter Ireland in future, when t'ey can speak again, t'at is.

Sparrow (*laughs nervously*) Um – well, excuse me – there's a question I have to ask. On behalf of my landlords. Um – is he actually living here by any chance, Mr Seamus – Mr O'Brien. O'Brien?

Bourke Oh yes, we're just a couple of Paddys living here, aren't we, Seamus? Just a couple of Paddys.

Blake Yes. (*Pause.*) Begorrah.

Sparrow Be – sorry, Mr O'Brien?

Bourke Begorrah. Yes, begorrah, is what he said. He's having a bit of trouble connecting thoughts to words. His head –

Sparrow And – is he here – on a permanent basis? Sorry, so sorry to pry like this but the landlords specifically insist that this is a one-person occupancy. The rent is agreed on that basis.

Bourke (*suddenly uncertain*) Well now, well now, sir, we're not sure of Seamus's plans since the incident at noon, are we, Seamus?

Blake Back to ta Emril Isle. Bloddy English. See.

Sparrow Mmm?

Bourke The Emerald Isle, t'at's Ireland, sir. Going back as soon as he can – because of te – te bloddy English, sir. Pardon me, sir, but in view of what's happened you'll understand –

Sparrow Yes, yes of course. And – and on behalf of my fellow countrymen, I'd like to apologise – and if by any chance he's still here when I come around next month, just, well – (*Winks.*) Make a point of being out, eh?

Blake Tanks.

Sparrow Now I'll get on with it – let you get to bed. (*Glances rapidly round room, checking off on clipboard.*) Bed, cupboard, chest of drawers, mirror, light bulb in place, bookcase, table, lamps, television set – functioning, I'm sure. (*Turns it on.*)

Voice on TV ... two hours ago of the spy, who was jailed for a record forty years. This is the most recent photograph that has been issued. The public are asked to report any sighting to their ... local police station, or contact Whitehall 1212 ...

Bourke Tat's moine that is! Paid for out of my own money.

Sparrow Oh, yes, you're right, quite right – it's not on the list. Oh, I'm so sorry. So sorry.

Bourke Are you?

Sparrow Yes, yes, very sorry indeed – well now, that's everything, thank you very much, goodnight, Mr O'Brien, Mr O'Brien.

> *He hurries to door, exits.*
> *Bourke and Blake stand staring after him, then turn to each other. Bourke lets out a howl of laughter. Blake yelps with feeble laughter.*

Bourke Begorrah, begorrah. Oh George, I never in my life heard an Irishman say 'begorrah'!

Blake But I'm not Irish, Sean. Half Egyptian, half Dutch. So naturally I say 'begorrah'.

Bourke And Emerald Isle – Emerald Isle – (*Laughs again.*)

Blake (*also laughing*) No, don't, Sean, please – please – my head!

Bourke Yes, the time's come for you to get what the good Dr Joseph ordered.

He leads Blake towards the bed.

A long rest. Sleep – she's right. That's what you need. And a lot of it.

Beginning to undress Blake.

Blake But we've only just put them on.

Bourke (*continuing to undress Blake*) But now the company's gone. So we can take them off, George.

Blake I may need – need to go to the lavatory, Sean. My bowels, you see –

Bourke That's all right, George. Call out when you want to go – I can help you to it.

Blake All evening I've needed – and now when I can – I can't.

Bourke But when you can I'm here. So don't worry about it, George. We're going to be living together closer than – closer than a husband and wife almost, almost, I mean less privacy than in the Scrubs even, so embarrassment doesn't come into it –

Blake The Scrubs! Wormwood Scrubs! I've finally left it, then, have I, Sean, thanks to you?

Bourke You have, George. And for ever. I'll see to it. Now you lie down –

He gets Blake between the sheets.

And close your eyes – close your eyes now. Try some of this – (*Begins to hum 'Danny Boy'.*) Always works with the English – the nice ones – Nigel and Annie and Dick and Philip – and even Miranda – I've seen their eyes fill with tears, even hers, so relax, George, relax – (*Hums more 'Danny Boy', croons it.*) There you go, George. You're off, aren't you, eh?

Blake murmurs from bed. Bourke goes on crooning 'Danny Boy'. Bourke gets up from beside Blake, wanders around room, humming. Sees tape recorder on table. Glances towards Blake in bed, then seizes tape recorder, presses 'Play' button.

Bourke (*voice on recorder*) – so allow as much as ten minutes at Halcyon Road lights to be certain – that you're not going to hit any major problems.

Bourke presses 'Stop' button, winds back, presses 'Record' button.

Bourke (*into recorder*) 'The Springing of George Blake. Chapter One. A Genius and a Gentleman.' That's what he called me. Well, I don't know about the gentleman – I hope I'm always a gentleman – of a sort – even as a thief. But a genius. Sheer genius, didn't he say? Begorrah! (*Laughs.*) But what matters is this. I've got George his freedom. And this. I've got myself a story to tell at last. A story to tell and a story to sell. They'll love me for it in Dublin – there I'll be . . .

Blake (*rears up in bed*) Sean, Sean –

Bourke (*turning off recorder*) What is it, George? You want the toilet? (*Going to bed.*)

Blake Promise me something.

Bourke (*sitting on bed's edge*) Anything, George. You know that.

Blake Get me to safety, Sean. Complete safety, please.

Bourke I've already arranged that. As soon as the time's right, I'm taking you home. To Dublin.

Blake No, no. *My* home. Get me to my home.

Bourke But – where is your home, George?

Blake Moscow. Moscow, please, Sean. (*There is a pause.*) Sean – you promised me anything.

Bourke But I don't know how to do it, George. I've got a plan worked out to get us to Dublin.

Blake What is it? What is your plan?

Bourke Well, you'll be under the kiddies' bunk in Nigel's and Annie's Dormobile, with Dick going along as extra camouflage, a little group of tourists, see, George, and I'll go separately, so there's no connection between us. Then we join up in Dublin –

Blake Moscow. Join up in Moscow. You and I.

Bourke But you can't keep yourself squeezed under a little bunk all across Europe to Moscow –

Blake Yes, I can. I can if I have to. Then you join me separately. Just as you said.

Bourke George, I've told you. I'm going to Dublin. I need to be there. Need to!

Blake Yes, yes, yes, you go home to Dublin – but come to me in Moscow first, Sean. For a short visit. A holiday. A week or two.

Bourke Oh, George, look at you, you should be lying down, you're trembling and shaking –

Blake You promised me anything! I want to go to Moscow. I want you to come separately, just as you said. Be with me a week. The thought of that, that'll help me survive under the bunk. Having you to look forward to, that's all I ask. Sean – my Sean.

Bourke All right, George. If that's what you want. I'll get you to Moscow. And come for a week myself. Just for a week I'll come. All right?

There are three short rings, one long one, on the bell. Bourke looks towards door.

Blake (*screams out*) I'm falling, I'm falling!

He grabs at Bourke.

Bourke (*holds him*) I've caught you, this time I've caught you, George!

Blake Gone, gone, gone, gone –

Bourke Hush now, George, hush, it's the signal, it's only Nigel and Annie, and Dick too probably, come to see you safe and sound! Let go of me, George, let go of me.

As again three short, one long ring on the bell. Lights.

SCENE THREE

Three weeks later. Moscow. Lunchtime. Dining room of Blake's flat. Table, chairs. Hatch to kitchen, off.

Stage left, Blake's room. Desk on which stands a typewriter, a pile of typescripts, and a very large and sturdy recording machine of the period.

Stage right, another room, similar layout to Blake's, a pile of typescripts on desk.

Blake is in his room, roaming about as he talks into the recording machine.

Blake (*his speech is slightly stilted*) And so at the age of seventeen, on the run from the Nazis because of my work in the Dutch underground, I managed to escape to England. Although I was born and bred in Holland, my father, being Egyptian, was entitled to British citizenship. As indeed was I. I therefore had no trouble in joining the British navy and was selected to be a member of the submarine service. (*He looks at his watch, sighs.*) Unfortunately, I soon discovered that the sensation of being under water filled me with the utmost terror. I applied, instead, for a post in the Foreign Office, and was immediately accepted. After the war I was sent to Korea. I will give an account of my experiences there in a separate chapter. But ideologically the most significant event of my life was when, back in London again, I was transferred to Intelligence and then to the Russian desk. I was put on a special course at Cambridge University – where all the top British traitors have always been educated (*stifles a slight laugh*) to study the Russian language, Russian culture, and the philosophical principles that lie behind the Soviet Revolution. One of my teachers was Tom Wingard, a senior civil servant. It was he who introduced me to the works of Karl Marx. 'Know Thine Enemy', his series of lectures was called. (*Looks at his watch again.*) An exceptionally objective, fair-minded man, he succeeded, without of course intending to, in converting me completely to Marxism. English teaching at its very best.

Zinaida enters carrying medals.

(*In Russian.*) Come in. News of Comrade Robert at last?

Zinaida (*in Russian*) Comrade Robert? No. Nothing.

Blake (*in Russian*) You've done a wonderful job, thank you, Zinaida.

Zinaida pulls him up to put the medals on.

(*In Russian.*) Not now, Zinaida. For the next official dinner.

Zinaida (*in Russian*) I want to see what they look like. (*She pins them on.*) There, now you are wearing what you have won.

Blake Yes. They positively glow with indecency and vulgarity. Best of all, they clink when I walk. *Spasiba*, Zinaida.

Zinaida *Zanyeshna.*

Zinaida goes into kitchen.

Blake Ah, yes, Tom Wingard. The memory of him brings me to the main point of this section of my book. That for those of us who worked steadily for the Communist cause, the Hitler–Stalin pact, the show trials, the summary executions, the internment, exiling or wholesale massacre of millions were indeed – (*pauses to find word*) sensitive issues. The struggle to reconcile our personal sense of what is just and right with our acknowledgement that there is a greater good at stake – a country of the future – is a painful one. But in the end that ideal, the country of the future, must prevail. The aphorism 'You can't make an omelette without breaking eggs' is often quoted. To which the frequent reply is: 'But supposing I don't want an omelette?' To this I can only say –

Viktor, carrying Bourke's suitcase, enters the dining room. He is followed by Bourke, who is followed by Stan, carrying Bourke's overnight bag.

Bourke Well, where is he, then? Where is George?

Stan He is probably in his study. Working.

Viktor Let us put your bags in your bedroom.

Stan And then we will find him.

Blake, medal still dangling half-attached, hurries into dining room, followed by Zinaida.

Blake At last! Robert!

Bourke Who?

Blake Well, here you are then.

Blake goes to Bourke, embraces him. Bourke responds.

Bourke Yes, here I am, George!

Blake Ah, Robert.

Bourke Robert, that's twice in two sentences you've called me Robert, George, don't you remember me? It's only been three weeks since you saw me.

Blake Robert's your – your *nom de guerre* while you're here – *nom de plume* as well, come to think of it. Don't worry – I'll explain it all to you when you've had a chance to settle. You'll be amused –

He throws anxious glances towards Stan and Viktor, who smile, nod.

I promise you.

Bourke What are those then, George?

Blake Oh, just – just a couple of gongs. Given for services rendered. Order of Red Banner. Order of Lenin. And this is Zinaida! My housekeeper. A jolly good one too. (*To Zinaida, in Russian.*) This is our guest, Comrade Robert.

Zinaida (*in Russian*) Comrade Robert. (*Nods.*)

Bourke (*attempting what he thinks is Russian greeting*) Comrobert. (*Then realising.*) Oh, Robert! Comrade Robert – that's me.

Blake Yes, you – (*In Russian.*) Can we have a bottle of champagne please, Zinaida?

Zinaida Of course.

There is an awkward pause.

Bourke And of course you know Stan and – and – (*Gesturing from Stan to Viktor.*)

Stan Oh yes. George knows us very well. We have become his great – great –

Viktor Chumps is the word. George's great chumps.

Stan No, no, chaps. We are great chaps.

Blake (*slightly obsequious*) No, Stan – I think the word you're both looking for is chums. We're great chums, the three of us. The four of us, I hope, Robert.

Viktor What then is a chump?

Stan I believe I know. A chump is a person who does something he knows is foolish. A mistake. (*Looks from Blake to Bourke.*)

Blake Yes, yes, an excellent definition, wouldn't you say, Robert?

Bourke (*watching closely but with an attempt at casualness*) That's right. 'Oh, what a chump!' we say. 'What a chump you've made of yourself.'

Blake Yes. 'What a chump you've –' But why are we all so formal? Let's sit down, um, chaps – (*laughs nervously*) like chums. Zinaida's gone to get us some refreshment, Stan, Viktor, Robert – champagne, you'll be glad to hear there's a plentiful supply of it, thanks to our excellent hosts – (*Almost bows to Stan and Viktor.*) And spirits too, mainly vodka, of course – but champagne's my favourite tipple –

Zinaida enters with tray, on it a bottle of champagne and glasses. She puts it on the table.

Russian, of course, but I've come almost to prefer it to the French, which I haven't drunk since my days in the British Consul in West Berlin and so can scarcely remember, but the Russian variety is fruity, earthy, it has a – a ripe peasanty fruitiness and pleasantness – (*opening bottle and pouring*) that I've come to – to prefer. (*Small, awkward pause.*) And as I say, there's lots of it – Oh, Robert, Robert! Robert!

Bourke (*gives a start, realising*) Oh sorry, yes, that's me, isn't it? (*Little pause.*) Yes, George?

Blake What was your journey like? I was getting quite anxious – wasn't I, Stan?

Stan Yes. He was afraid you had changed your mind about coming.

Viktor We would not have liked that, Robert.

Blake So what was it like, your trip to Moscow?

Bourke (*assumes a tone of jolliness, glancing nervously from face to face as he speaks*) Well, George, as it turned out, it was the loveliest trip of my life – 'Have you anything to declare?' asks the man at Victoria Station. 'Only a pint of scotch,' says I, 'and that's inside me' –

Laughs. Blake, Stan and Viktor laugh.

– and stamp they go, on my false passport. I got one in the name of Kennedy, George K. Kennedy – I mean, what's the point of spending five years in the Scrubs if you don't know how to get a false passport in the name of George K. Kennedy to take you to where you don't want to go?

He laughs. Stan and Viktor look at Bourke blankly.

Stan Where you don't want to go?

Blake There, that's what I was telling you about, the Irish sense of humour, they love anarchic jokes, jokes that *seem* hostile –

Bourke Oh Jesus, yes, chaps – (*Laughs again.*) That's the joke I always made to myself every time I approached a new frontier, out of terror, you see. But I needn't have

34

worried, because stamp they go in Calais, and stamp they go in Berlin – stamp, stamp, stamp, stamping me and old George K. right through Checkpoint Charlie –

Stan Stamp?

Viktor You put it on an envelope? Or walk heavily, stamp, stamp –

Blake No. On your passport. (*Makes passport-stamping motion with his fist.*)

Stan (*in Russian*) You have his passport?

Viktor (*in Russian*) I forgot to take it.

Bourke What? A problem –?

Blake Viktor was just saying to Stan that he forgot to take your passport.

Viktor Yes. My mistake. Can I have it, please?

Bourke My passport?

Stan We have another one for you.

Viktor And it is not forged.

Bourke Oh. Well, in that case –

Takes passport out of his pocket. Viktor takes it, hands him new passport. Bourke studies it.

But it's – what is it? I can't make it out.

Stan It's Ukrainian.

Viktor With your name on it. Robert Adamovich Garvin.

Bourke Robert Adamovich –

Viktor Garvin.

Blake Which is why I've been calling you Robert, you see, Robert.

Bourke Robert Adamovich Garvin, eh? (*Makes to put passport into his pocket.*)

Viktor Please permit me, Robert.

Takes passport from him, puts both of Bourke's passports into his pocket.

Bourke But – but I don't get to keep it, then? Not either of them?

Viktor It remains in possession of the Department.

Bourke But when I go home. I mean, how do I –?

Stan It is returned to you.

Bourke Oh. Well, I suppose that's – that'll do. As long as I can get it when I need it. But it's a little strange, George. For me, I mean. Here I am, one minute Sean Bourke, with a false passport of my own, and the next I've got a genuine passport in somebody else's name – Robert Adamovich something – and the next I haven't got any passport at all. (*Laughs anxiously.*) If you see. A little strange, eh? (*Little pause.*) George?

Blake Yes. Yes, I know. But – well, they want to keep your identity concealed, Robert. There are spies all over Moscow. British, American, West German. They're bound to discover I'm here. Any day now. Isn't that right?

Stan It is inevitable. A certainty.

Blake (*referring to Stan and Viktor*) And then if they discover I'm being visited by an Irishman called Sean Bourke, late of the Wormwood Scrubs – well, that will lead them to Nigel and Dick, also late of the Wormwood Scrubs. And then to Annie. And Philip. And Miranda – Dr Joseph – they'll all go to jail. We don't want that. Do we?

Bourke No. No, of course not.

Stan We are very grateful to you and your friends for all that you have done for us. You have brought George Blake here. To us.

Viktor You must not be punished because of it.

Bourke No. Thank you. You're right –

Blake The George that's here – this George – (*passing the glasses on tray*) wants to propose a toast.

Holds up glass. Others follow suit.

To Robert Adamovich Garvin! Without whom this George – the George that's here – wouldn't be here!

Viktor *and* **Stan** Robert Adamovich Garvin!

They drain off their glasses.

Bourke Thank you, thank you.

Stan Now (*rising*) I have to go home. To arrange for my wife's aunt's husband's funeral.

Blake Oh, I'm sorry, Stan. Very, very sorry. My condolences to – to your wife. To . . . Katerina.

Stan Oh, she is happy. He was not a nice – chap – you see. In fact, he was a complete chump. Shouting, swearing, drunk, violent. Often I wanted to –

Points finger at Bourke, makes soft shooting noise.

Viktor (*who has also risen*) I must go home too. My daughter is taking part in her school's display of gymnastics. She is gifted but dumpling. I tell her, 'Starve, my child, starve and become famous and rich.' But like most childs –

Stan Children.

Viktor Yes, of course, yes, children – like most children she likes to lie on the cushions listening to pop, and who can blame her? I tell you who. Her mother. Also me. (*Laughs.*) So –

Stan So. So welcome to Russia, Robert.

Shakes Bourke's hand.

Viktor Yes, welcome to Moscow. I hope you will be at home with us.

Shakes Bourke's hand.

Bourke Thank you, I am, I feel I am. Thank you.

Blake Goodnight, comrades. See you soon. And thank you for all – all you've done for us.

Bourke Yes, thank you.

Stan (*in Russian, to Blake*) How is the book coming on?

Blake (*in Russian*) Oh, I keep working on it.

Stan nods.

Viktor (*in Russian*) If you need any help –?

Blake (*in Russian*) Perhaps when I get to the end –

Stan and Viktor go out, calling 'goodnights' to Zinaida, who returns them.

Bourke What was that? The Russian bit at the end?

Blake They were asking about my book.

Bourke Your book?

Blake Yes. They want me to write my autobiography. They think it'll be a great propaganda coup.

There is a pause.

Bourke So, they're your publishers too, are they? As well as being whatever it is they are.

Blake No, they're not my publishers. What they are is officers of the KGB. Rather high-ranking ones. At least, they outrank me.

Bourke KGB?

Blake Yes, KGB.

Bourke I see. (*After a pause, makes an effort.*) But what about your own trip, George? How was that?

Blake (*absently*) The worst thing was my bladder. Nigel and Annie – no, it was Dick – only gave me the one bottle. I filled it before we got to Calais, so from then on – well, there were times when I thought of giving myself up, just so I could have a pee. I shouldn't have asked you to come. (*Little pause.*) I shouldn't have been so – so – damned selfish. (*Little pause.*) I shouldn't have persuaded you to come.

Bourke (*little laugh*) Well, can you explain further?

Blake They don't trust you. Stan and Viktor. And the committee of the KGB.

Bourke Committee? What committee?

Blake Their job is to analyse your every move, every word. Every aspect of your behaviour. As observed and reported by Stan and Viktor.

Bourke Like a parole board, you mean?

Blake Oh, they're far more powerful than a parole board. Parole boards can only keep you where you don't want to be. But Stan, Viktor, the committee, they can –

Bourke (*after a little pause*) What, George?

Blake points finger at Bourke. Makes soft shooting noise.

That's twice in no time I've been shot with a finger and a hiss.

Blake Yes. But they don't always use fingers for shooting. And never when they mean it. They use bullets in the back of the neck. If ever a chap owed a chap an apology –

Bourke In this case it's a matter of a chap and a chump. I knew it was the wrong thing to do. Knew it in my blood and bones!

Blake I didn't. Not for a second. If I had, I wouldn't –

Bourke I know, George. Is there anything stronger –? (*Indicating champagne.*) You mentioned vodka, wasn't it?

Blake goes to hatch, raps on it. Zinaida raises hatch.

Blake (*in Russian*) A bottle of vodka, please, Zinaida.

Zinaida passes out vodka, vodka glass.

Thank you.

Zinaida closes hatch. Blake opens bottle, pours vodka into glass, hands it to Bourke, puts bottle beside him. Bourke downs vodka, pours more, downs that.

Bourke What do they suspect me of? Why don't they trust me, George? After what I've done for them?

Blake Well, to understand it, you have to look at it from their point of view. Supposing they had a top Western agent in one of their high security prisons. And somebody comes along – a Ukrainian – a single Ukrainian fella called Robert Adamovich Garvin, let's say – and the top Western agent saws through a few bars, the single Ukrainian fella, Robert, throws a rope ladder over the wall, drives him around the corner to a flat in Moscow, and then hides him in the bunk of a Dormobile and gets him driven to London. To them the idea is preposterous. Because they can't begin to understand what it means to have incompetent liberal Englishmen for your masters, half-witted and uneducated Englishmen for your jailers, and above all a single Irish fella for your friend –

Bourke But why? Why do they think the single Irish fella would do it?

Blake One possible explanation – you're a British agent. Planted in Wormwood Scrubs to make friends with me, get me out. With the concealed connivance of the British government. Then you follow me to Moscow. Pick up names. See how the KGB really works – then off to Ireland, and in due course back to London for a debriefing. Unfortunately they have a very high regard for British Intelligence.

Bourke But you told them – Stan and Viktor and this KGB committee – you told them it was your idea I come here for this – this holiday?

Blake Of course.

Bourke They don't believe you?

Blake They believe I think that's what's happened. They also believe it's possible you manipulated me into thinking that's what happened. That's their world, you see, Robert. That's how they're paid to think. It's how they earn their pensions.

Bourke And what is it I have to do, George? What exactly do I have to do, to survive?

Blake The most important thing is – to be natural. Then it's mainly a question of don'ts. Don't ask questions. Don't snoop – not that you would. But don't *look* as if you're snooping. Avoid picking up any Russian. You'll start using it. Then they'll suspect you're already fluent in it. Keep yourself innocently occupied.

Bourke What, sightseeing, holidaying, being a tourist? I can do that all right, I'm looking forward to it.

Blake You won't be allowed out much, I'm afraid. When you are, you'll be accompanied by Stan or Viktor or both. No – the solution is work.

Bourke Work! What sort of work?

Blake Editorial work.

Bourke Editorial work! (*Laughs, in spite of himself.*)

Blake (*also laughs slightly*) It was my idea. I pointed out that you edited the Wormwood Scrubs in-house magazine, so why didn't you help turn some of their translations of political tracts into grammatical and idiomatic English? Stuff with titles like *Tractors, Wheat and Bread: A History of the Economic Revolution in the Ukraine and Belorussia* – stuff like that, making it readable. You can do that, Robert. Easy-peasy.

Bourke I can make it grammatical and idiomatic. I doubt I can make it readable. (*Laughs.*) It's the vodka.

Blake What?

Bourke My thinking it'll be all right. I'll get out of this and through to Dublin.

Blake Of course you will, Sean – no, Robert – no, Sean, damn it! Tonight, at least, you're Sean. And look, Sean, we've already got out of a worse pickle than this one! So to us, Sean! To Sean and George! (*Raising glass.*)

Bourke (*also raising glass*) To George and Sean! And anyway, what's all the fuss? My being a good boy – see nothing, hear nothing, say nothing – for a week, that's all it amounts to.

Blake Six months, Sean.

Bourke stares at him.

They want you to stay for six months.

Bourke Oh, Jesus.

Blake To give themselves time to watch you. Listen to you. Satisfy themselves that you are who and what you claim to be. And actually are. As I know. A single Irish fella –

Bourke Six months! Six months of – of acting natural? Every minute of the day? Here? In Moscow?

Blake Yes. That's the – the sentence, so to speak, Sean. You'll do it standing on your head. I know you will.

Bourke George – George – I believe I've got to lie down for a while. I've gone a bit dizzy –

Blake (*getting up*) Here. Let's get you to your room. (*Picks up Bourke's bags.*) You rest until dinner. Zinaida's a terrific cook – her chicken casserole is scrumptious.

Bourke Good, George, good. I'll – I'll look forward to that then. Her chicken casserole.

Blake leads Bourke into Bourke's room, puts down bags, turns suddenly, and emotionally.

Blake It's going to be all right. I'll look after you. What you've been to me, I'll be to you. We're in this together. As always. Trust me. Please, Robert.

Holds out his hand, takes Bourke's.

Bourke (*taking Blake's hand*) Of course I trust you. It's Sean, though. Sean for tonight, George. Isn't it?

Blake Yes. Sean, Robert.

Bourke Oh Jesus, oh Jesus, oh Jesus!

Looks at bag, fumbles to the bottom, pulls out tape recorder, presses 'Rewind' button, stops, presses 'Play' button.

Bourke (*voice on recorder*) I really believe this to be true- – that nobody in the whole bloody world could have done what I've done! I, Sean Bourke –

Bourke presses 'Stop' button, presses 'Record' button.

Bourke (*into machine*) This is probably madness, absolute madness.

He stuffs recorder back into bag, crouches furtively over concealed machine.

Just the sort of thing George's warned me against – see no, hear no, speak no – And I wasn't going to anyway, not during the little week I was here, this was just going to be an exotic aside in my story, visiting George all safe and sound in Moscow, the two of us in our pomp – but I've already said this, before I left I said it, that first evening out of the Scrubs I said it, I knew in my blood and my bones it was a mistake. I had the chance, all I had to say before he ran out of the flat and down to Nigel's and Annie's Dormobile was, 'Sorry, George, I've changed my mind, I won't be coming to Moscow, home to Dublin for me – and see you – see you some time –'

Lights dim slightly as he goes on speaking, inaudibly. Blake, meanwhile, has gone back to the dining room, picked up the champagne bottle and glass, gone on into his study. Pours himself a glass of champagne, takes a sip, presses 'Rewind' button, then 'Play' – it is inaudible to audience – rewinds. Presses 'Record'. As Bourke becomes inaudible:

Blake (*into recorder*) No, it's not a question of whether you want an omelette. The egg always gets eaten in some form or other. Or it rots and is thrown away. The thing is to make sure that as many who live, are allowed to live, have an egg, cooked in some fashion, to eat. Sacrifices *are* inevitable for the greater good. Otherwise there's no point to my having done what I've done. That doesn't mean, it does not mean, that there is pleasure to be found in doing what has to be done to those for whom no eggs are available, no eggs allowable, or what is done, indeed, to the egg itself – it is a hateful business, a dreadful habit but I – I insist that I – and others like me – who saw the light, had no choice, no choice but to follow our –

Lights dim slightly on him as he speaks inaudibly and intensely towards machine.

During this Zinaida comes out. Begins to lay table for dinner. Lights fade slowly on Bourke crouched over machine in his bag; Blake roaming around room as he speaks into his machine; Zinaida laying table.

Curtain.

Act Two

SCENE ONE

Six months later. After dinner. Bourke and Blake are sitting slightly away from each other. There is an atmosphere of tension. Bourke has vodka in front of him. Zinaida is finishing the clearing up.

Bourke (*clears his throat, looks at Blake's chest*) I see it's a night for the medals, George.

Blake Yes, I promised Zinaida this morning.

Zinaida, catching her name, glances towards him. Blake smiles vaguely towards her.

As it gives her so much pleasure and costs me so little effort – (*Gestures coldly.*)

Bourke I've never worked out why they mean so much to her. As if she'd won them herself.

Blake Because she's very proprietorial, Robert. Like most Russian servants. A legacy from the serf-owning days. The serfs owned the masters as completely as the masters owned the serfs.

Zinaida looks from Bourke to Blake anxiously, goes to kitchen.

The same was true of the slaves in the southern states of America, from all historical reports.

There is a tense and ghastly pause, during which Zinaida looks through hatch, draws it softly down.

Bourke (*in a sudden panic*) Excuse me, George, excuse me – (*Getting up.*) Won't be a minute –

Hurries to his room.
   *Blake watches his exit coldly. Bourke pulls out bag
from under bed, bends over, speaks into tape recorder.*

What's going on, that's what I want to know. Something's
going on, as sure as hell's hell. It's never been like this
before, he's never been like this before – Look, look,
here's something I'm going to say that could be the death
of me, but that's what I'm talking about, fretting about,
isn't it? The death of me – because that's what it's like,
like waiting for my own death – so if anything happens to
me before Tuesday, or on Tuesday itself come to that –
if any accident befalls me, so to speak – Oh, shut up,
Robert – Sean – Sean, nothing's going to happen, boyo,
nothing's going to 'befall' – and if it does there's nothing
you can say now will help you then, so calm down,
calm down – go back and do what you've done this
last six months, go back and act natural and don't say
another word, don't think another thought about
Tuesday. Tuesday's Tuesday and will turn up in due
course. Preferably on Tuesday, eh? So keep away from
mentioning Tuesday as if your life depended on it.

   *Laughs, puts machine away, makes to go to door,
stops, goes off. Sound of lavatory flushing. Bourke
comes straight out into dining room.*

Sorry about that, George, being taken short like that.
A touch of trouble with the old stomach.

Blake Would you mind shutting the door properly,
Robert? Your door.

Bourke Oh, right. Sorry, George.

   *Closes door, goes back to chair, sits. Picks up glass,
drains contents. Pours himself more. Blake watches
him.*

Blake (*as Bourke raises glass to his lips*) That can't be

47

doing it any good. Your old stomach. You're making it older by the glassful, Robert.

Bourke You're right, George. Dead right.

Puts glass down, undrunk. Blake raises his glass of champagne, sips from it.

Look, George, what is it? Is it what I said about Tuesday? Going home on Tuesday. If I did, it was accidental, George, and not meant to be detrimental. Not to you, of all people. Did I say anything accidentally detrimental to you, George? If so, I apologise.

Blake What you said was that I'm lacking in normal, human feelings.

Bourke I couldn't have said that, George! I couldn't have!

Blake Not in those actual words, of course. You didn't actually say, 'George, you're lacking in normal, human feelings.' But it was the implication of what you did say.

Bourke Which was what? What did I say?

Blake takes a sip of champagne, is silent.

Oh, come on, George – (*Cajolingly.*) What did I say, tell me what I said and I'll apologise for the implications. How's that for a deal, George?

Blake (*gets up, goes to his study door*) I must get back to my work. (*Stops.*) What you said actually, Robert. What you actually said. After you'd congratulated yourself on your good fortune in escaping from my adopted country, my flat and my company on this coming Tuesday – what you actually and actually said was: 'It's a good thing for you, George, that you never suffer from homesickness. That you can brush your past aside without another thought.' That's verbatim, Robert.

Bourke (*after a miserable pause*) I don't believe I said 'brush', George. I believe I said 'push'. And I didn't mean, the last thing I meant –

Blake (*coming back*) What you meant, Robert, was what I've already stated you implied. That I'm some sort of emotionless – (*gestures*) freak. But hasn't it occurred to you, Robert, hasn't it ever occurred to you that the reason I'm not homesick is because I'm finally at home? Morally and spiritually at home. Which is the only kind of home worth having. For me. (*Little pause.*) My past was always in the future. The country of the future. This is where my feelings have always been. Does that mean I have no feelings, Robert? Does it? But of course you've never understood –

Bourke Oh Jesus, George, I understand – I understand better than any man alive that you're as human as they come. I mean we've been close, as close as two men could be. I'll never forget you in your concussion back there in London, so helpless, dependent, vulnerable you were, George, but the one thing you fixed on – the only thing you fixed on was getting yourself here.

Blake With your help, of course.

Bourke However. You'd have done it however, George. With me or without.

Blake No, I wouldn't have, Robert. Helpless, dependent, vulnerable. I needed you as a man needs his wife. Didn't I?

Bourke (*shocked*) What, George?

Blake Well, isn't that what you said at the time? Mumbled it into the fog and headache of my concussion – that you were looking after me as if you were my wife. Or as if I were your wife. Which way around was it, Robert, come to think of it?

Bourke I don't remember, George.

Blake Don't remember whether you're my husband or my wife? (*Little pause.*) Oh come, Robert, it's usually quite easy to distinguish between the one and the other – especially in a shortish marriage like ours, eh?

Bourke Whatever I said was just a way of speaking about our friendship, George. However I behaved, it was as your friend. (*Little pause.*) What's the matter with you, what's the matter? I've never seen you like this before!

Blake I loved my wife. I still do.

Bourke Oh, I see, I see. Yes – well, you know, you don't talk about her, so people forget, I forget –

Blake Silence on certain personal matters doesn't necessarily come from a lack, Robert. Of normal human feelings. My Madeleine still is, and ever will be, my Madeleine. If she'd had her way she would have stood by me for the whole of my sentence. For every one of my forty years. Or at least as many as she would have survived. Her health is so delicate – she's always afflicted with some sort of rash, on one part of her body or another – and the heroic manner in which she endured her almost constant conjunctivitis. It was I, Robert, I who insisted on releasing her from her vows. For her sake. For the sake of our three children. About whom, you may have noticed, I also do not speak.

Bourke That's why I forget you had them – have them.

Blake The knowledge that my Madeleine has embarked on a second, equally successful, marriage gives me joy. Not pain. She deserves to live under another name, legally acquired. With a man who isn't, and is unlikely ever to become, a jailbird. (*Pours himself champagne, raises his glass.*) Madeleine, dear wife of my heart and my loins. Mother of my beloved children, I salute and honour you – the ladylike embodiment of all the womanly virtues, including the finest virtue – domestic loyalty.

Bourke, hurriedly and amply filling his glass with vodka, raises it.

Bourke To Madeleine. The perfect embodiment.

They clink glasses. Blake begins to shake, then lets out a howl of laughter. Bourke stares at him in bewilderment, then, realising, also lets out a howl of laughter. They rock and shake with laughter.

Oh, Jesus – Oh, Jesus, George –

Blake Oh God, oh dear God –!

Bourke I thought you'd gone mad on me, George. Around the bend, I thought you'd gone, and out of sight.

Blake Although of course the fact that I don't think about them doesn't mean I wouldn't love them if I did think about them.

Bourke But there's no point if you can help it. She's gone. And they're gone. The kiddies.

Blake Kiddies. They're not kiddies, Robert. They're children. My *children*. Please.

Bourke Sorry, George. Children.

Blake And one day I might even see them again. Who knows? And I wonder what I'll make – or they'll make – and on Tuesday, Robert. It's been quite hard for me. To think of you – your heart and mind intent on Tuesday. As if you're being released from prison at last. The prison of me. You've put in your six months. And so now –

Bourke Oh, George! That's not it!

Blake You had the same spring in your step, the same roll to your gait, the same *joie de vivre*, humming, singing, almost prancing and dancing, when you were doing your last few days in Wormwood Scrubs. And of course trying not to let me see it – out of delicacy for my feelings. A delicate chap, is our Robert. (*Nods at him.*) When it comes to feelings.

Bourke Not delicate enough, it seems. It's not you I'm wanting away from, George. Ever. It's just the need – the need to be home again. You know that. Like some animal, wounded animal –

Blake Yes. Some wounded animal. Lolling about in the pubs of Dublin.

Bourke laughs, slightly shamefaced.

Lionised you'll be, won't you? That's the only animal part of your future, Robert. (*Smiles at him.*)

Bourke I'll stay on a little longer, if you want. A few days. A week even.

Blake Oh dear God, this is awful! Awful! (*Paces about in agitation.*) Help me, Robert! Help me!

Bourke How, George? How can I? Even if I stay on a bit, our time is up.

Sound of door opening. Stan's and Viktor's voices in the hall, greeting Zinaida in Russian.

Blake (*under his breath*) Oh, damn! Damn, damn!

Bourke looks at him, confused. Stan and Viktor enter. There is a tense pause. Stan and Viktor look enquiringly at Blake.

(*In English.*) Stan. Viktor. Good evening.

Stan George. Robert.

Viktor Good evening, Robert, good evening.

Stan Good evening.

Bourke Haven't seen you two for a while. How's everything on the Western front? (*Laughs awkwardly.*) Home front, I meant to say.

Stan (*attempting easiness – badly*) Oh, my wife's recently widowed aunt has moved in with us. I begin to understand now why her late husband drank and beat her. She is a terrible nuisance. (*Laughs, shakes his head.*)

Bourke Who was it said, 'Nobody ever left me anything but relatives to look after'? Dickens, wasn't it?

Stan Dickens?

Bourke Charles Dickens. Wasn't it, George?

Stan Oh, Charles Dickens! Yes. A great writer. Much worshipped. Here. In Russia.

Bourke Yes, I've seen his books when you've taken me out to the shops. Well, I think they must be his, because there's his photograph on the back. (*Laughs.*)

Viktor Still making no progress with our language then, Robert?

Bourke No, my eyes go funny when I see the letters, and my hearing goes off when I listen to the sounds. Not a word, not a word – but Ludmilla, how's her sprained ankle, Viktor?

Viktor Completely cured. So she's probably thinking how to sprain the other one. She's too fat now to be anything but a thrower of the discus.

Stan Discus thrower.

Viktor Yes. Of course. Discus thrower. So perhaps I'll put her on steroids. For the next Olympics, eh?

There is laughter. Then another tense pause.

Well, George? What's the situation?

Blake What will you have?

Raps on the hatch.

Tea, coffee, a glass of champagne?

Stan Nothing, thank you. We're here for a minute only. To see how everything is.

Blake Are you sure?

Stan Yes.

Zinaida enters. She looks to Stan and Viktor. Both shake their heads, grimly. Zinaida makes to go out.

Blake Ah! – but there's one thing. Zinaida – just a minute! (*Turns to Bourke. In English.*) Robert, give them a performance, Stan and Viktor! Robert may not have learnt any Russian but – go on, Robert.

Bourke Oh now, George, I don't think Stan and Viktor –

Stan Oh, no. Please. (*Gestures politely.*)

Viktor Yes. Please. Whatever it is.

Bourke hesitates, then begins to croon 'Danny Boy' at Zinaida. Zinaida, anxious and embarrassed, looks from Stan, to Viktor, to Blake.

Blake (*in Russian*) Please, Zinaida. The comrades want to hear you.

Stan and Viktor nod unenthusiastic encouragement. Bourke starts 'Danny Boy' again. Zinaida joins in. Bourke drops out, leaving Zinaida to sing through, charmingly, words incomprehensible to her, to the end. Stiff laughter and applause from Bourke, Stan, Viktor, Blake.

Stan (*in Russian, to Zinaida*) Thank you, Zinaida. Now please leave us.

Zinaida runs off to the kitchen, giggling with pleasure and embarrassment. There is a pause.

(*In Russian, to Blake*) Well, it's obvious that you haven't told him.

Blake (*in Russian*) I was just about to. When you turned up. (*In English.*) It was going to be my next sentence, Robert. Or next but one. If Stan and Viktor hadn't appeared. You see.

Bourke What?

Blake Stan and Viktor. And their committee. Don't want you to go back to Ireland on Tuesday. Nor – nor – in fact, nor in the immediate future, Robert.

Bourke (*after a pause*) But we had an agreement. Six months was the agreement. And they're up. My six months is up.

Blake Things have changed, Robert.

Bourke Changed? Changed how? Why?

Stan They found the car you left in – in – (*Looks at Viktor.*)

Viktor Harvist Road.

Stan Yes. And they've traced it to you. They have your name. Photographs. Your prison record. They know everything about you.

Viktor Except where you are.

Bourke But – what does it matter if they know who I am, or where I am, as long as I'm in Dublin?

Stan You'd almost certainly be extradited to Britain. To stand trial.

Viktor The committee has taken expert legal advice –

Bourke I don't believe it, Viktor. I know my own people. They'd never give me up. Not to the old John Bull. They wouldn't.

Blake They would in the current political climate, Robert. You wouldn't be a political refugee, you see. Just a criminal. On the run. I do know about these things. My years in the Consulate – you'd be extradited.

Bourke Well – well, that's my risk. I'm ready to take it.

Stan But you wouldn't just be taking it for yourself, Robert.

Viktor You'd be taking it for all those people who helped you in London.

Blake Nigel and Annie. Dick. The doctor –

Bourke But even if I'm extradited – which I don't accept – I don't accept – you're not thinking I'd give their names to the English police? I'd die before I betrayed Annie and Nigel. And – and the rest of them. You know that, George!

Stan We *all* know that, Robert. But you wouldn't only be having deals with the English police. Not once they know you've been to Moscow. Met Viktor and me. Stayed with George. No, you would be having deals with very different sorts of people. Believe me, Robert. One of our agents in London – not even an important one – when they'd finished with him – (*Gestures to Viktor.*)

Viktor I visit him every month. One of my duties of compassion. He is in a clinic. He will be in the clinic for the rest of his life. His nervous system is so 'no hope' that he is almost a complete – what word? (*Says Russian word for 'imbecile'.*)

Stan Fool. Idiot. Silly person.

Blake Imbecile.

Viktor Yes. Thank you, imbecile.

Blake Not at all, Viktor.

Viktor Sorry? Yes? What – ah – (*Confused.*) Yes, Teodor. Poor Teodor. He can no longer arrange the chess pieces on the board. He was our champion, Robert. Chess champion of the KGB. The imbecile. (*Shakes his head sadly.*)

Stan We do not want this to happen to you, Robert.

Viktor You are too precious to us.

    There is a pause.

Bourke Well, well – I was just saying to George. I can stay on a few more days. A week. A few more weeks. (*Pause.*) Well then – well then – how much longer? I could do another month. Time for the dust to settle. (*Looks at their faces.*) Two even. (*With an effort.*) Three?

Blake It will have to be years, Robert.

Bourke Years, years, how many years? How many?

Blake Five, Robert.

Bourke (*in a whisper*) Five years! (*Staring around at their faces.*) But what do I do here – what do I do – for another five years? Eh, George? (*Little pause, then supplicatingly.*) George?

Stan We will assist you to pursue a career in publishing. For which you have great gifts, Robert.

Viktor Yes, who is this droll chap from the Ukraine, our Moscow publishers ask. Who is this Robert Adamovich Garvin, who makes such excellent and witty corrections to our old-fashioned English translations.

Blake Well, there you are, Robert. Witty and excellent. Words that equally applied to your editorship of the Wormwood Scrubs house magazine. I doubt that they'll ever be applied to my own literary effort. I sound like a pompous liar. In every sentence I – (*Shakes his head.*)

Bourke (*interrupting*) It's not the – the notion that I might do a book of my own, is it? These extra five years?

There is a pause. Blake, Stan, Viktor look at each other, as if puzzled.

Stan What do you mean, Robert? Haven't we explained?

Viktor We're thinking of you. And your friends.

Bourke Still, I want you to know – and your committee to know – that not a word of my part in George's escape will come out when I get home. As far as I'm concerned all the glory can belong to the KGB. All right? And here's my hand on it.

He holds his hand out to Viktor, who shakes it. Then to Stan, who shakes it. Then to Blake – then withdraws it.

No, I don't have to do this with you, do I, George? It would be an insult to the two of us.

Blake Yes, it would. Though yours is a hand I always like to shake, Robert. In almost any circumstances.

Holds his hand out to Bourke. Bourke takes Blake's hand. They shake, solemnly.

Bourke Thank you, George. Well, there we are then. That's settled then. All understood and cleared up. Your real worry you don't have to worry about.

Stan (*beaming*) I shall pass your undertaking straight on to the committee. You will publish nothing about George's escape.

58

Bourke That's it.

Viktor And you agree to remain with us for another five years.

Bourke No. No.

Blake It's all settled then, Robert.

Bourke No.

Blake All settled, Robert.

Stan Our thanks, Robert. On behalf of the KGB.

Viktor Speaking in person, Robert, I'm glad you agree to stay with us. I would be sorry to lose you. You bring us much funniness.

Stan (*to Blake*) Fun is the word, yes?

Blake Yes. No. Well, he brings us both.

Bourke Fun and funniness I bring you, do I? For the next five years. Thank you. (*Laughs dully.*)

Stan You have made a wise choice.

Embraces Bourke.

Viktor Yes. Very wise.

Embraces Bourke.

Stan (*in Russian*) We will talk about your book, George. Very soon.

Viktor (*in Russian*) If I can give help –

Blake (*in Russian*) Thank you. Goodnight.

Stan *and* **Viktor** (*in Russian*) Goodnight.

Go out, calling 'goodnights' to Zinaida in Russian en route. She answers them. There is a pause.

Bourke So you knew all the time. And you couldn't tell me.

Blake I can't tell you how badly, how badly I feel –

Bourke You feel. *You* feel. But I'm the one who's doing the facing here, the facing of five years, so let's talk for once about my feelings here, George. About them. Let's talk about *them*!

Blake Yes. (*Little pause.*) Well – let's talk about them. Your feelings.

Bourke I haven't got anything to say. You know my feelings.

Blake Yes. One thing, though. Why I so much wanted you not to want to go so much – was that you wouldn't mind so much being obliged to stay. You see.

Bourke (*laughs*) Very daintily put, George. Very daintily put.

Blake What I mean is – what I mean is! That I didn't want you to go for my sake. As I've already made clear. But by God, by God, Robert, I did want you to go for your sake. I wanted *that* far more. Far more than what I wanted for myself. Do you think I don't know I owe you that? Do you think I don't know you deserve it! All I've ever wanted since you got me out of Wormwood Scrubs is to pay you back. And all I've succeeded in doing is to trap you in a plight that gets worse. And worse.

Bourke Oh well, what the hell. (*Laughs.*)

Blake (*looks at him, astonished.*) What?

Bourke You've got your bad feelings, I've got my five years, but when you come to look at it, George, the last six months – we've had good times, a lot of laughs.

Blake Yes. We have.

Bourke And there may be something in this publishing career Stan and Viktor are urging me into. I'll learn everything there is to know about the business. When I get back to Dublin, five years from now, I'll set up on my own. Control the Russian market. That's how I've got to look at it. I'm going to spend the next five years teaching myself a good business. Making a future for myself. I choose – yes, that's it – I *choose* to spend my next five years here. And as I'll be spending them with you, George –

Blake They'll pass in a flash. I'll see to it.

Bourke We'll have more good times, George. (*Raises his glass.*)

Blake To more good times! To all the more good times!

Blake hesitates, then comes into Bourke's open arms.

Bourke Goodnight, George. Till tomorrow. Until tomorrow. The start of a new day. (*Picks up the vodka bottle.*) By way of a new dawn.

Blake A new dawn. And a new day.

They separate, go to their rooms. Pause at their doors. Turn. Look at each other, make to speak, nod and smile at each other. Blake sits down at his desk, very still. Thinking. Bourke goes straight to the tape recorder, presses 'Record' button, makes to speak straight into it, microphone in one hand, vodka bottle in the other, turns machine off, sits, in distress, thinking. Blake leans forward, stabs 'Record' button, speaks.

Every time I hear the words 'treacherous' and 'deceitful' applied to me I find myself reflecting on those groups of men who in their day were similarly described and with whom I have much, I believe, in common. Those Roman Catholic priests, say, who during the Reformation were not thought to be just wicked or evil, but were – like me – thought to be agents of the Devil himself. Like me, they were forced to go about their life's tasks in secret. Like me, their purity of intention was only preserved through many forms of duplicity. A sacred duplicity of the heart and of the soul in the name of their God, as they like me, and I like them, sought to bring about a Kingdom of Heaven on earth. (*Little pause, as he loses control of the line of thought.*) Let me proceed with this thought. But do I have to proceed with this thought? What is it about, this thought? It's about justifying the betrayal of the man who brought me out of captivity, back into life and freedom. The only man who could have done it. The single. Yes, the single Irish fella did it. Did do it. (*Little pause.*) How ridiculous. Ridiculous that I should –

He turns off the machine, sits, thinking.
Makes to start machine again. Stops himself.
Bourke simultaneously makes to start machine, stops himself. Raises vodka bottle to his lips. Notes that it's almost empty.

Bourke Hah! That's it, that's it, of course that's it!

Goes out, strides to hatch, bangs on it.

Zinaida, Zinaida! Zin, Zin!

Zinaida opens hatch, sees Bourke, grins.

Zinaida (*in Russian*) Another vodka?

Bourke (*in English*) Another wodka. Yes. Another wodka. Please, Zin.

Zinaida vanishes then re-enters and plonks a bottle of vodka in front of Bourke, who grabs it.

That's my lovely Zin. Here's what we're going to work on. Starting tomorrow, my Zin, Zin of my heart. My darling. Here's one to drive any sane man to his doom.

*Begins to croon 'When Irish Eyes are Smiling'. Zinaida
stares at him, transfixed. Blake makes to speak into
machine, stops, stares towards dining room, as
Bourke's voice rises to higher and higher notes on
'When Irish Eyes are Smiling'.*
    Lights.

SCENE TWO

*Blake enters, in overcoat and hat. Blake looks at Bourke,
the table, in disgust.*

Bourke Morning, George. (*Pouring himself a vodka.*)

Blake Actually, it's the afternoon. Still at your breakfast,
I see.

Bourke Only just begun it.

Blake (*indicating typescripts*) What's all this doing in
here?

Bourke Oh, it's become such a muddle in there (*nodding
to his room*) I've decided to spill over. I hope you don't
mind.

Blake Actually I do.

Bourke (*catarrh*) Sorry, George.

Blake I do wish you'd confine yourself to your own sty.
I'll have Zinaida clear up – Stan and Viktor will be here
for lunch shortly.

Bourke And where have you been, George?

Blake Out. For a walk.

Bourke Cold, eh? From the look of you.

Blake Very. But it helped me to think. About you. About
what's happening to you.

Bourke What's happening to me, Georgie?

Blake Sorry? What did you call me?

Bourke Georgie.

Blake I'd rather you didn't.

Bourke Why not?

Blake For one thing it's not my name.

Bourke Well, it's a hell of a lot closer to your name than Robert is to mine. But I'll tell you what – if you let me call you Georgie, you can call me Bobbie. (*Chuckles.*)

Blake Do you know what you're beginning to remind me of? One of those lifers in Wormwood Scrubs. The ones who'd given up all hope.

Bourke God, I love the ways you say 'Wormwood Scrubs' in, Georgie, always the whole name. ''Member that summer, '58, '59, Bobbie, delightful old place, what was it, Shrubs something Shrubs, no, no, Scrubs, that was it, wasn't it, Bobbie, Wormwood Scrubs, delightful accommodation – if a touch cramped – splendid grounds, a mite inaccessible and the staff, Bobbie, in their splendid uniforms –' (*Laughs.*)

Blake (*watches him*) I came back with a resolution, Robert. A resolution that I'd help you. As a matter of urgency, actually. The greatest urgency. I was going to try to talk to you as we used to talk – remind you of the publishing opportunities you were so eager to pursue, the need to keep at these properly – (*indicating typescripts*) to put on your best front with Stan and Viktor so they'd start reporting back favourably to the committee –

Bourke Oh, bugger Stan and Viktor. Bugger their committee too. If I can't live where I want, I'll live how I want. And how I want is like this. See.

Blake Nevertheless I shouldn't – if I were you – let Stan and Viktor see you like this. Not today. Especially not today. I'd go in and spruce up and sober up. If I were you.

Bourke Well, you're not, are you, Georgie! You're not me! And that's the whole difference between us!

Blake And it's one I'm devoutly grateful for . . . Listen, Robert . . . Is that one of my cigars?

Bourke Yes, it is. Thank you, Georgie.

Blake Have you been in my study?

Bourke I just popped in to see how things were.

Blake goes into his study. Picks up books from the floor, puts them on bookcase. Rewinds tape recorder and plays it.

Blake (*voice on recorder*) . . . the most sophisticated eavesdropping devices then in existence. Which of course brings me to the Berlin tunnel. The Berlin tunnel was – was – oh, this is unendurable. I can't go on with this –

Bourke (*voice on recorder*) Don't worry, George, I'll do it for you. I've heard it from you so often, I know it by heart. Here we go, George. (*Imitating Blake's voice through this.*) The Berlin tunnel, my tunnel as I call it because of the significant part I played in its establishment as a nerve centre for treachery, was undoubtedly the greatest achievement of the propaganda war, providing information from the Germans to the Russians, who gave it back to the Americans, who passed it on to the Turks, who handed it to the Chinese who gave it back to me. And of course the true triumph of it all was that everything that passed from country to country was a pack of lies that concluded with forty thousand top spies in the pay of their Western masters being lined up against

65

the walls of their respective cities and being mowed
down. Apart from one or two who were tossed alive into
their department furnaces, and roasted before the terrified
gaze of their colleagues. *Pour encourager les autres*, so to
say. (*Imitates Blake's laugh.*) I spurned such glory as
came my way–

> *Bourke pours himself another drink, looks at it, puts
> his glass on the table without drinking, in a gesture of
> disgust.*
> *Zinaida has come back into dining room to clear up.
> Bourke, glancing with apprehensive triumph towards
> Blake's room, puts his arm around Zinaida's waist.*

Bourke Come on then, Zin, Zin, Zin, come on, my old
darling, let's have it.

> *Begins to croon 'When Irish Eyes are Smiling'. Zinaida
> struggles, alarmed, looking towards Blake's room.*

You sing, my girl! (*With ferocity. Croons again.*)

> *Zinaida, fearfully, starts singing along with Bourke.
> Blake looks towards their voices, makes as if to go to
> door, checks himself, goes back and, with an air of
> determination, rewinds tape recorder. As he does so,
> he opens bottle of champagne, pours himself a glass,
> takes a sip as he presses 'Play'. Listens to Bourke's
> parody. He stands for a moment, thinking, then begins
> to laugh, turns off machine. Goes into dining room,
> carrying glass of champagne. He smiles at Bourke and
> Zinaida.*
> *Zinaida falters.*

Blake (*encouragingly*) No, finish, finish please.

> *Zinaida and Bourke sing to the end. Blake toasts
> Zinaida. Then, in Russian:*

Thank you, Zinaida. Now if you'd go to the kitchen –

Zinaida goes into kitchen.

Well, it did occur to me. But I couldn't quite believe it. Now it all makes sense.

Bourke Really? What makes sense, George?

Blake Your deterioration. It's deliberate. An act.

Bourke No, it's not an act.

Blake But it's deliberate.

Bourke I hope so. (*Puts his hand to his head.*) And I hate every minute of it. But you had to see what I could do. When I put my mind to it.

Blake But I already know what you can do, Robert. Who better?

Bourke Yes. But you had to experience the living with it, didn't you? I mean, there was no point my saying I'm going to fill every corner of your life with my disgust-ingness – I had to fill it. And today, George, I've really begun – I'll go on and on and on – every day for the next four years, nine months – and I'll get worse. Believe me, George. I'll get so much worse that I won't even have to try. It'll be first nature.

Blake Unless?

Bourke You know what unless.

Blake You really think Viktor, Stan, the committee – they'll put up with it?

Bourke What difference does it make to them? They don't have to live with me.

Blake So you think I can just go to them and say, 'For God's sake, send him back to Ireland. I can't tolerate another minute of him in my flat. My life.'

67

Bourke That's my belief. It has to be. Otherwise I'm without hope. A lifer –

Blake You – without hope! I've seen you do five years in Wormwood Scrubs – (*Nods ironically.*) The Scrubs.

Bourke That was then. I'm older now. George – believe me. Please. I've got to go home.

Blake You might. Even now. If you bring all your resilience, your determination –

Bourke I'll put them to just one end, George. Making your life insufferable.

Blake God! It's not a question of my getting them to send you home, it's never been that, it's a question – I told you, I told you right from the start, it's been a question of – of saving your life, Robert. I was hoping I wouldn't have to tell you this. That's what I was doing this morning. I wasn't out for a walk, I was begging Stan and Viktor to beg the committee to let you live.

Bourke What?

Blake In the name of God, Robert, go and make yourself presentable. Please.

Bourke (*shakily*) This is serious, then?

Blake It couldn't be more serious. When I left it seemed on a knife-edge. They're not letting me have any part in the decision. Come on, hurry. Hurry!

They go into Bourke's room.

Bourke But why, why, why now, after they've got me here?

Blake They still don't trust you. And then from what they've seen of you recently, and from Zinaida's reports of your drinking –

Bourke Zinaida!

Blake Of course. Surely you realised that! She goes into the department once every two days –

Bourke Oh Jesus, not Zinaida.

Blake It's not her fault. She's employed by them. She gives an exact tally of how many bottles you've drunk, describes the state of your room, your behaviour – and of course I couldn't argue with any of it, could I – not when they've seen for themselves? They think you're, well, even if you're not a double agent, they do believe that you've become unstable. And are therefore a security risk.

Bourke And so they're going to kill me. Kill me.

Blake I don't know, I don't know what they'll decide – it's the picnic factor, you see.

Bourke Picnic factor?

Blake They may just be coming around to inspect you. (*Inspects him.*) And at least you're not in your underwear and that dressing gown this time – and we can keep it up from there, can't we? I mean, from dressed to respectable, hard-working –

Bourke Oh Jesus, George, yes, yes. Yes. But this picnic factor –?

Blake If they say, let's not be dull and have lunch here, let's go to one of the KGB's dachas and have a picnic, I'm to say – I've been ordered to say – that I would rather stay here, at home, and work on my book.

Bourke And – and I go on the picnic. (*Raises his finger, points it, makes shooting noise.*) Is that what you mean, George?

Blake I don't know, I don't know. Perhaps they won't know themselves until they've got you in the dacha and

69

observed you on your own without me to – to protect you.

Bourke And if I refuse to go?

Blake Refuse to go on a picnic? With the KGB? (*Suddenly remembering.*) Oh, God –

Bourke What, what!

Blake The tapes! Your voice. If they hear your voice on the tape.

Bourke Wipe it, George, please wipe it . . . Please! Please!

Blake All right.

Blake goes out to his room, winds tape back, etc.

Bourke Thank you, George . . . Jesus! I've got to get out of here. Now.

Pulls on overcoat, crams vodka bottle in pocket, seizes bag with tape recorder, hurries out. As he does so, sound of front door opening. Stan's and Viktor's voices greeting Zinaida. Zinaida returning greeting. Bourke stands frozen. Stan and Viktor enter.

Stan Oh hello, Robert. All ready then?

Viktor Well muffled up, that's good. Though the dacha is quite warm –

Stan We're lucky to have got it for the afternoon. One of our best.

Viktor We're going on a picnic. Didn't George tell you? If we could get a dacha – pity he won't come too. All work, no play, makes boy a dull John.

Stan No, no – makes John a dull boy, isn't it, Robert?

Bourke Jack, Jack, a dull Jack – (*Moving towards door.*) Makes Jack a dull boy – I'm not going on any picnic. I'm not going on any bloody picnic with the KGB.

Bourke bursts past Stan, opens the door, hurls himself outside, slamming door.
Curtain.

SCENE THREE

Six weeks later.

Blake (*sitting at desk*) . . . but I used to be good at waiting. I mean . . . all those years of waiting to be caught and tried for my crimes, so-called – sometimes it was as if my crimes were merely what I did while I was waiting to be caught and tried for them. And I waited with complete serenity through my trial and sentencing. And patiently in jail until you came to get me out – but the truth is, I never knew what waiting was, Robert, until this last six weeks. It's a very painful thing to have to do – real waiting. And in a few minutes, just a few minutes . . . now in fact.

Bourke enters main room from front door. Dishevelled and clutching his bag, he bangs on the hatch.

Bourke Zin – Zin!

Zinaida enters, upstage left, stares out at Bourke.
Blake looks towards dining room, stands up.

A bottle please, Zin – wodka, wodka.

Zinaida (*in Russian*) Oh, you poor man, you poor man – look at you!

Bourke (*urgently*) Wodka please, Zin.

Zinaida hands Bourke a bottle of vodka, staring at him, shaking her head anxiously and pityingly. Bourke opens bottle.

Thanks, Zin, my old darling. Thank you.

He takes a long swig. Blake comes out of his room. Zinaida closes hatch.

Blake So here you are then.

Bourke Been expecting me, have you?

Blake Every day for the last six weeks. But with confidence this evening. A traffic policeman spotted you going into a barber's shop.

Bourke Yes. That was the last of my roubles. But I couldn't stand all that growth. I've been clean-shaven all my life. I've been short-haired all my life. And I figured that if I was coming back to it at least I'd come back to it looking as I usually do. My face, anyway. (*Little pause.*) So they know, do they, Stan and Viktor? Know I'm back?

Blake Oh, yes. They've been called out of some big function. That's how important you are, Robert. You're a much wanted man, you see.

Bourke And they're on their way over, are they?

Blake They are. As always when they're least wanted, eh? And where have you been, these last six weeks?

Bourke Out. And about.

Blake Out and about where, exactly?

Bourke In the woods, mostly.

Blake In this weather! But where did you sleep –?

Bourke Under newspapers. Nothing else I could do. No passport. Almost no money – started turning into a tramp. By tomorrow I'd have been a beggar as well. But hard to be a beggar if you don't know the basic words, like 'money', 'food', 'help'. (*Laughs.*) Have to stand there, on street corners, silent, with my hand out. And your boys would have seen me, in the end. So – so why wait, why wait, George? (*Looks at Blake.*) In that condition, why wait?

Blake (*after a little pause*) I see you clung on to your – (*Nods to bag.*)

Bourke My what?

Blake Your machine.

Bourke takes out recorder, tapes. Pushes them at Blake. Blake hesitates.

May I? (*Winds back, presses 'Play'.*)

Bourke (*voice on recorder*) . . . truth of it is, I need to hear a voice – a voice in my own language – no, the truth of it is I need to hear *his* voice. I've heard it every day for years now, it's become a part of me, a part of my life. God, how I miss him, God, how I miss it, God how I miss him. Even though it's because of him that I've come to this. I dream – almost every night I dream of them there. George and Zin, my darling Zin. And even Stan and Viktor, and in my dreams it's like – like my family – Zin! Wodka, wodka, another bottle, please. (*Laughs.*) Another bottle, please. George, my friend, help me, help me!

Blake turns off machine, puts it and tapes into Bourke's bag.

Bourke (*in person*) How long have you known?

Blake Well, when I saw you talking into it in London. The first day – the day you got me out.

Bourke And that's when you planned to get me to Moscow. And to keep me here. Or did you already have it in mind when we were in the Scrubs – and we were discussing how I could help you escape? Did you, George?

Blake I can't remember, Robert. But I might have. Even in the Scrubs I was an officer of the KGB. A prisoner of war, so to speak. So I had to consider all the possibilities.

Bourke Like the possibility of betraying me.

Blake Spies betray people, Robert. That's what we do. It becomes a – a habit. Difficult to break – even when it's not – not strictly necessary.

Bourke (*nods to bag*) So it's always been the book that you've been afraid of?

Blake Well, it does make us seem absurdly incompetent – that the KGB couldn't do what you did. A single Irish fella. With his rope ladder and the Dormobile.

Bourke But they didn't even try, did they, George? That must be a galling thought, eh?

Blake It has been now and then. Yes.

Bourke And what's the authorised version going to be?

Blake We don't know. We can't work it out. I can't, anyway. Every time I try to write it up I get – (*shrugs*) stuck.

Bourke Well, now I'm going to be out of the way, you'll unstick yourself, probably.

Blake Yes, well this brings me to the – the little matter I should have started with. You see, what happened that morning, six weeks ago – what happened –

Sound of door opening. Stan and Viktor enter, greet Zinaida.

(*To himself.*) Oh, damn! Damn, damn!

Bourke sinks to his knees, lowers his head.

Stan What is this – Robert, what are you doing?

Bourke I want my picnic here. Now. In front of him.

Stan (*in Russian*) So you haven't told him? (*In English*) On your feet please, Robert. On your feet.

Bourke So this is what you wear for an execution.

Viktor Robert. This is for the dinner.

Stan The reunion dinner. The KGB reunion dinner. Full uniform always.

Stan Why didn't you tell him?

Blake It must have been – shame, I think.

There is a pause.

Stan Well, tell him now. Listen to him, Robert. You will hear the truth. I guarantee it.

Blake What I was about to tell you, Robert, was that there was never any question of killing you. I – I made all that up. I knew Stan and Viktor were going to invite you on a picnic. In a dacha. And I – used it.

Bourke (*after a pause*) Why?

Blake To – well, I suppose, to teach you a lesson. A – a small counter-ploy. Your ploy was to turn yourself into something unspeakably less than yourself. So my counter was –

Bourke To be yourself.

Blake As I said – it's a hard habit to break. I never expected you to run off like that. I thought you'd spend a few terrified hours in the dacha and then come back relieved to be alive, and then you'd, well, knuckle down. I should have known better, shouldn't I?

Stan Go on, please, George.

Blake As for the KGB committee – Stan and Viktor – they never had the slightest intention of forcing you to stay. Not for five years. Not even for the six months.

Stan We hoped you'd stay. We wanted you to stay. We argued – that's all – argued with you to stay. But force – against your will? Never.

Viktor Also we liked your company. You are very Russian. To us, Robert, you are the cat's knees.

Stan Bee's whiskers. Finish now please, George.

Blake I am instructed by my superiors to offer on behalf of the KGB profound apologies for my behaviour.

Stan Now everything is understood at last. Yes, Robert?

Bourke What is understood – what I understand – what I think I understand is that I'm free to go.

Stan Exactly. A free man. You always have been.

Viktor But we would like you to stay. Would prefer it.

Bourke Now. I want to go now, please.

Stan Very well. It will take a few days to arrange your travel.

Bourke But go from here now. This place.

Stan I understand. We will find you a hotel – (*Looks at Viktor.*)

Viktor The Union Hotel. The Department has a suite there. For important guests.

Stan The Union Hotel. (*Nods.*)

Bourke I need to be away – need to. This very minute.

Stan Then this very minute we go.

Blake (*in Russian*) You realise he'll publish his book.

Stan In English, please, George.

Blake You realise, he'll publish his book.

Stan Then he publishes his book. (*To Bourke.*) We don't want you to. But we can't stop you. And won't try.

Viktor Though you did make a promise –

Stan In the wrong circumstances. He thought he had no choice. Robert knows our wishes. He will decide for himself.

Blake (*in Russian*) But – but you can't – (*Catches Stan's look. In English.*) Do you really want to go to the Union Hotel? Looking as you do. And, well, smelling as you do.

Stan (*to Bourke*) The Union Hotel will be honoured to have you.

Viktor Yes, I'll make sure of that.

Blake Please – stay, Robert. Just for a few days. So we can – can talk – one last time at least, please, Robert.

Bourke The name is Sean. Sean Bourke. Sean Alphonsus Bourke.

Blake (*picks up Bourke's bag*) Don't forget this, Sean.

Hands it to Bourke. Bourke goes out, followed by Stan and Viktor. Blake stands as, from the hall comes:

Bourke Oh, Zin – I must say goodbye to my darling Zin.

Stan (*in Russian*) The comrade is leaving.

Viktor (*in Russian*) He wants to say goodbye.

Zinaida makes gasping, wailing noise.

Bourke Now don't take on, my Zin, don't take on – just one more time – for old times' sake.

Bourke croons 'Danny Boy'. Zinaida joins in. Bourke laughs.

And a last cuddle. There. Don't take on so. Think of me from time to time, eh . . . Goodbye, George.

Sound of steps, front door closing. Blake stands for a moment. Goes to hatch, knocks on it. Zinaida opens hatch. She is dabbing at her eyes with apron.

Blake (*in Russian*) Zinaida, a bottle of champagne, please.

He walks to his room. Sits down at desk. Zinaida appears, carrying bottle of champagne and a glass on tray. Enters. Puts down fresh bottle and glass, picks up empty bottle and other glass.

(*In Russian.*) Thank you, Zinaida. Oh – (*making an effort at contact*) my medals. (*Picks them up.*) Would you like to give them a polish?

Zinaida brightens slightly. Breathes on medals, rubs them on her apron, looks at them, shakes her head, puts them on tray, goes out. Blake opens bottle, pours himself a glass. Takes a sip. Looks at tape recorder, rewinds, presses 'Record'.

(*To machine.*) To the question, in other words, of whether I have in my conscience – in my heart – any remorse, any regrets, I give this answer: how can I have remorse or regrets when I have devoted my life's work to mankind? And thus have the privilege, indeed the honour of being where I am now. Here. Here in this country of the future.

Presses 'Stop', stares ahead. Picks up champagne glass, holds it out in toast.

To the country of the future!

Raises glass to lips. Blackout.

Curtain.